Book 1

Python Crash Course

By: PG WIZARD BOOKS

&

Book 2

Fortran Crash Course

By: PG WIZARD BOOKS

Book 1

Python Crash Course

By: PG WIZARD BOOKS

Step By Step Guide To Mastering Python Programming!

Python Crash Course: Step By Step Guide To Mastering Python
Programming!

Table of Contents

Introduction

Learning a programming language can be a daunting task for many, but the right guidance can be the differentiator and the ultimate deciding factor as to how well you learn the language. Python is an easy to learn, high-level language which supports both structured and object-oriented programming.

This book aims at making the basic fundamentals of the language clear to the programmers. The dynamics of the language have been explained so as to enable developers to learn fine coding skills. Python has readable codes and an easy syntax thus making it simple to learn. It has automatic memory management system along with a comprehensive library that allows the programmers to write programs in a fewer lines of code as compared to other programming languages like C++ and Java.

Learning Python can be your stepping stone in the field of programming since Python methodologies can be used in a broad range of applications.

Lastly, the book is useful both for beginners who want to master this language and the experienced programmers who wish to revisit the basics or want a manual for reference. We would like to thank you for downloading this book and we hope that the book is valuable for its readers.

Chapter 1: Preamble to Python

Python programming language was created by Guido Rossum in 1989. It is an object-oriented, multi-purpose and interactive scripting language. The language has been designed as highly readable. Python has fewer syntactical constructions and uses English keywords frequently. It is considered as a great language for beginners in the programming field.

Features of Python

1. Python provides rich data types and easier to read syntax as compared to other languages.
2. As compared to other programming languages it allows more run-time flexibility.
3. It is a platform independent scripted language with complete access to operating system API's.
4. Python libraries are cross-platform, thus making them compatible with Windows, MacIntosh and Linux.
5. It supports interactive mode that allows snippets of codes to be tested and debugged interactively.
6. It is a portable language and can run of various hardware platforms with same interface.
7. The Python source code can be easily maintained.
8. It provides support and an enhanced structure for big programs than shell scripting.
9. For building large applications, python can be assembled in to byte-code.
10. Python can be effortlessly incorporated with JAVA , C++, C , COBRA and Active X.
11. It can be used for programming video games, various scientific programs and artificial intelligence algorithms.
12. It has automatic memory management system.

Python is a self-sufficient language and consists of many tools and once the programmer becomes aware of their uses then it becomes an easy task for them. The language makes a solid foundation to branch out and learn other programming languages.

Python Crash Course: Step By Step Guide To Mastering Python
Programming!

Installing and Setting Up Python

Python distribution is available for wide range of platforms. It is easy to install and nowadays many Linux and Unix distributions include the latest version of Python. To download and install Python you can visit http://www.python.org/downloads/ and opt for the desired version. Even though version 3 is the latest but still Python 2 is used widely. Once you have downloaded and installed you need to set up the path. To add the Python directory for a particular session in-

Linux /UNIX –

a) In the csh shell type setenv PATH "$PATH:/usr/local/bin/python" then press Enter.
b) For   Linux,   in   the   bash   shell,   type   export   ATH=
   "$PATH:/usr/local/bin/Python" then press Enter.
c) Type PATH="$PATH:/usr/local/bin/Python" in the sh or ksh shell and press Enter.
d) Please note that /usr/local/bin/Python is the path of the Python directory.

Windows-

a) Type path %path%;C:\Python at the command prompt and press Enter.
b) The path of Python directory is C:\Python

Running Python

There are three different ways to start Python. Python can be started from DOS, UNIX or any other system that gives you a shell window or a command-line interpreter. You can right away start coding in the interactive interpreter-

```
C: > python #Windows/ DOS
Or
python% #Unix/Linux
or
$python #Unix/Linux
```

A python script can be executed at command line by invoking the interpreter on your application.

IDE – Integrated Development Environment

You can run Python from GUI (Graphical User Interface) environment as well, provided you have a GUI application on your system that supports Python.

1. IDLE is the very first Unix IDE for Python.
2. For Python, PythonWin is the first Windows interface and is an IDE with a GUI.
3. From the main website the Macintosh version of python along with IDLE and IDE can be downloaded either as BinHex's files or MacBinary.

Make sure the Python environment is set up properly and is working fine so that you can execute your codes easily. (Python - Environment Setup)

Chapter 2: Basic Syntax

In the previous chapter, we learned how to install and set up Python. This chapter we will discuss the Python Syntax. A set of rules that defines how a program will be written and interpreted is called Syntax.

Let's understand various methods of programming

Interactive Mode Programming

At the command prompt type the below mentioned text and press Enter

print "Hello, Python!"

The output in version 2.4.3 will be *Hello,Python!*. Incase you are using the new version then you will have to use parenthesis along with the print statement–

print ("Goodmorning, Python!");

Script mode programming

The execution of script begins and continues till the script the finished upon invoking the interpreter with script parameter. As soon as the script finishes the interpreter will not be active any more. To understand it better take a look at this simple program.

Python files have extension **.py.** Type the source code *print "Hello, Python!"* in a test.pyf file and try to run the program as - *$ python test.py.* It will generate the following output –

Hello, Python!

Now presuming the availability of Python interpreter in /usr/bin directory, run the program as-

$ chmod +x test.py   # to make the file executable

$ ./test.py

Output will be –

Hello, Python!

Identifies in Python

A name which is used to recognize a variable, class, function, module or other subject in Python is called as an identifier. An identifier begins with a to z or A to Z letters or a _ (underscore) which is followed more letters or a zero, digits (0 to 9) and underscores. No punctuation characters like %, $, @ are allowed within Python identifiers. It is a case dependent language.

a) Class names begin with uppercase letters and all other identifiers begin with a lowercase letter.
b) An identifier which begins with a single foremost underscore indicates that it is private.
c) An identifier with two leading underscore denotes a strongly private identifier.
d) The identifier is a language-defined special name in case it ends with two trailing underscores.

Reserved Words

There are certain reserved words in Python which cannot be used as variable or a constant or any other identifier name. All reserved words are in lowercase only.

not	exec	and
or	finally	assert
pass	for	break
print	from	class
raise	global	continue
return	if	def
try	import	del
while	in	elif
with	is	else
yield	lambda	except

Lines and Indentation

In Python, to indicate blocks of code for function and class definitions or flow control, there are no braces. The line indentation denotes the block of codes. In the indentation, the number of spaces is variable, but inside the block same amount of indentation should be done for all statements. Therefore, a block is formed by all the unbroken lines which have been indented with same number of spaces.

Multi-Line Statements

A new line in Python typically marks the end of a statement. However, the use of line continuation character (\) is allowed to denote the line should continue. Example –
Total = goods_one + \
     goods_two + \
     goods_three + \
The line continuation character is not required for statements contained within brackets ( ), [ ] or { }.

Quotation

In python, all three quotes (' , " or """) are accepted. These indicate string literals provided the same kind of quote begins and closes the string. To cover the string across multiple lines, triple quotes are used.

Comments

The comment in Python begins with a hash (#) sign that is not within the string literal. After the hash all characters up to the end of the physical line form a part of the comment. However, they are ignored by the Python interpreter.

Blank lines

Blank lines are ignored by Python. These are the lines which have just whitespace, probably with a comment.

Multiple Statements on a Single line

On a single line multiple statements are allowed with a semicolon (;) provided that none of the statement starts a new code block.

Suites

In Python, a single code of block made by a cluster of statements is called as suites. The compound statements like if, else, while, def and class need a suite and a header line. The header lines start with statement (including keyword) and a colon denotes the end. They are trailed by one or more lines that make a suite.

Chapter 3: Python Fundamentals

Now that we know the syntax of Python, it is imperative for programmers to understand the python fundamentals. In other words, we would be discussing the basics on which the Python programming is based.

VARIABLES

A reserved memory location where values are stored is known as a variable. Memory space is allocated by the python interpreter and on the basis of data type of a variable it takes decision on what to store in this reserved memory. Hence, in the variables storing of characters, integers, or decimals is possible by assigning them different data types.

How to assign values to variables?

For assigning values to the variables you need to use the equal (=) sign. The left hand side operand denotes the variable name and the right side operand denotes the stored value inside the variable. Example –

counter = 10   (integer assignment)
miles   = 100   (floating point)
name   = "Tom"   (string)

print counter
print miles
print names

In the above example-10, 100 and Tom are the values assigned to counter, miles and name variables respectively and will give us the result as –
10
100
Tom

Assigning a lone value to numerous variables at the same time is also possible.

Example –
x= y= z= 1

In the above example, with value 1, the integer object is created, and same memory location is assigned to all three variables. Apart from this multiple objects can also be assigned to several variables. Like –

x, y, z = 1, 2, "Tom"

Data types

There are many types of data which are reserved in memory such as; age of a person is defined in numbers, and his address is defined as alphanumeric. To define the operations possible there are several standard data types which are used. We are just writing a brief on them as of now and these will be explained in detail in next chapters .They are –

a) Numbers – As the name suggests numeric values are stored in this data type. Upon assigning a value to them number objects are created. Various numerical types that supported by Python are–

(1) Signed integers (int) e.g. – 2, 4, 44 etc.

(2) Long integers (long), they can be depicted in hexadecimal and octal as well. e.g.- 0122L, -0x19323L etc.

(3) Floating point real values (float) e.g. – 5.0, 2.22, -88.88 etc.

(4) Complex numbers (complex) e.g. – 3e+26j, 45.j etc.

b) Strings –The adjoining set of characters depicted in quotation marks are called strings. Both single and double quotes are allowed in Python. The concatenation operator is represented as plus sign (+) and the repetition operator is represented as (*) asterisk.

c) Lists – These are mainly flexible data types in Python. The items in a list are separated by a comma and are written inside square brackets. The concatenation operator is represented as plus sign (+) and the repetition operator is represented as (*) asterisk.

d) Tuples - It is data type in sequence, similar to lists. A comma separates the number of values contained in tuples and unlike lists they are enclosed in parenthesis. Lists cannot be updated.

e) Dictionary – Dictionaries in Python are hash table types. They function like hashes or associative arrays and consist of key-value pairs. The dictionary keys are typically numbers or strings. The curly braces enclose the dictionaries and by using ([ ]) square brackets values can be accessed and assigned. For example, to create, add and delete entries in dictionary

```
# make a phone book:
phonebook = {'Tom Halter': 665544, \
'Liza Raymond': 889966, 'Ronald Johnson': 776655, \
'Kim Lee': 443344}

# add the person 'Mathew Peterson' to the phonebook:
phonebook ['Mathew Peterson'] = 99887766

del phonebook ['Kim Lee']
```

OPERATORS

The constructs which can manipulate the value of an operand are known as operators.

Python operators

1. Arithmetic

These operators execute various arithmetic calculations like addition, subtraction, division, multiplication, exponent, %modulus etc. For arithmetic calculation, there are various methods in Python like you can use the eval function, calculate and declare variable, or call functions.
Let us take a simple example –

```
a = 4
b = 5
print a + b
```

Output will be "9". Similarly other arithmetic operators like division (/), multiplication (*), exponent (**) etc. can be used.

2. Comparison

The comparison operator compares the value on either side of the operand to determine the relation between them. Various comparison operators are (!=, ==, >, <, <=, >=).

Example – we will compare the value of a to the value of b and print the result in true or false. Assume value of a =4 which is smaller than b =5. Now when we print the value as a >b, it actually compares the value of a to b and since it is incorrect, it returns as false. Similarly you can use other comparison operators.

3. Assignment

To assign the value of the right operand to the left operand, we use assignment operators.They are (+, +=, -=, /=, *=, %=, **=, //=). Example-

num1 = 4
num2 =5
print ("Line1 – Value of num1:" , num1)
print ("Line2 – Value of num2:", num2)

Output –

('Line1 –Value of num1:',4)
('Line2 – value of num2:', 5

4. Logical

These operators are used for conditional statements which are true or false.
AND, OR and NOT are the logical operators in Python
AND – it returns TRUE if both left and right operands are true.
OR – it returns FALSE if either of the operand is true.
NOT – it returns TRUE if operand is false

Example-
x = true
y = false
print ('x and y is', x and y)
print ('x or y is', x or y)
print ('not x is', not x)

The result will be –
('x and y is', False)

16

('x or y is', True)
('not x is', False)

5. Membership

Inside a sequence such as strings, lists or tuples membership is checked by these operators. These are of two types (in and not in). These operators give result based on the variable present in specified string or sequence.
Example –
We will check whether value of x=3 and y=7 is available in list or not by using membership operators.

x= 3
y =7
list = [1, 2, 3, 4, 5];

if (x in list):
   print "Line 1 – x is available in the given list"
else:
    print "Line 1 – x is not available in the given list"

if (y not in list):
    print "Line 2 – y is not available in the given list"
else:
    print "Line 2- y is available in the given list"

Result of the above code –

Line 1 – x is available in the given list
Line 2 – y is not available in the given list

6. Identity

Memory locations of two objects are compared by identity operators. They are of two types – is and is not.
is – it returns true if two variables point the same object otherwise false.
is not- it returns false if two variables point the same object, otherwise true.

Example –

17

x = 10

y = 10

if (x is y):

       print "x & y SAME identity"

y = 20

if (x is not y):

       print "x & y have DIFFERENT identity"

Following result is generated –
x&y SAME identity
x & y DIFFERENT identity

7. Bitwise

A bitwise operator work on bits and performs bit by bit operation. Python supports the following Bitwise operators - & Binary AND, | Binary OR, ^ Binary XOR, ~Binary Ones Complement, << Binary Left shift and >> Binary Right shift.

Operators Precedence

It determines which operator needs to be evaluated first. Precedence of operators is necessary to avoid ambiguity in values. For example – multiplication has a higher precedence than addition. Following operators are usedin Python – (**, ~+ -, */ % //, + -, & , ^|, >><<, &, <=<>>=, <> == !=, is is not, in not in , not or and)

STATEMENTS

Anticipating the conditions that might occur while executing a program and specifying the actions according to those conditions is called decision making. The decision structures assess numerous expressions which produce TRUE or FALSE as a result. You need to determine which action to take and what statements to execute if the result is TRUE or FALSE otherwise. In Python programming any non-zero and non-null values are assumed as TRUE, and if it is either null or zero then it is assumed as FALSE value.

Following types of decision making statements are provided in Python –

1. **if statements** - it contains a Boolean expression followed by one or more statements.

    A logical expression is used to compare the data and decision is made on the basis of comparison result. If Boolean expression evaluates to TRUE, then the block of statement(s) inside the *if* statement is executed. In case it evaluates FALSE, then the first set of code after the end of *if* statement is executed.

    Syntax –
    if expression:
      statement(s)

2. **if....else statements** – In this an *if* statement is followed by an optional *else* statement. If the conditional expression in the *if* statement resolves to FALSE value or 0, the block of code executes in an else statement.

    Syntax –
    if expression:
      statement(s)
    else:
      statement(s)

3. **elif statement** – It permits you to examine multiple expressions for TRUE and carry out a block of code as soon as one of the condition evaluates to TRUE. They are also optional statements and random number of *elif* statements following an *if* can be there.

    Syntax –
    if expression 1:
      statement(s)
    if expression 2:
      statement(s)
    elif expression3:
      statement(s)
    else:

19

statement(s)

4. **nested statements** – When you want to examine a different condition when a condition works out to be true then you can use *nested if* statements. Inside a nested if statement, an *if...elif ... else* inside another *if...elif..else* construct is also possible.

Syntax –
if expression1:
    statement(s)
    if expression2:
        Statement(s)
    elif expression3:
        statement(s)
    else:
        statement(s)
elif expression4:
    statement(s)
else:
    statement(s)

Chapter 4: Learn about Python loops, Strings, Lists, Tuples, and Dictionary

We have already introduced these terms in the previous chapter. Now we will take a look at each one of them in detail so that you can understand their usage in Python programming.

LOOPS

Typically the statements are executed in sequence, but if a situation arises when you are required to execute a block of code many number of times. In Python, a loop statement permits you to execute a statement or a group of statements numerous times. To handle the looping requirement following types of loops are available in Python –

1. **while loop** – this loop repetitively executes a target statement as long as the condition given is true.
   Syntax-
   while expression:
      statement(s)

   Here, it can be a single statement or a block of statements and the condition may be an expression. The loop iterates as long while the condition is true. When the condition becomes false, the program control passes to the line immediately following the loop.

2. **for loop** – these loops have the capability to iterate over items of whichever sequence, like a string or list.
   Syntax-
   for iterating_var in sequence:
      statement(s)

   The sequence which contains an expression is evaluated first and then the first item in a sequence is assigned to the *iterating_var*. After this the statement block is executed. All the items in the list are assigned to *iterating_var*, and the statement(s) block is executed until the entire sequence is exhausted.

3. **Infinite loop–** If a condition never becomes FALSE it becomes an infinite loop. The results in a loop that never ends are called as infinite loops. These loops might be useful in client/server programming where server needs to run continuously for the client programs to communicate with it as and when required.

Using else statements with loops

If an else statement is used with for loop, then the else statement is executed when the loop has exhausted iterating the list. When else is used with a while loop, the else statement is executed when the condition becomes false.

Loop Control Statements

The execution from normal sequence is changed with loop control statements. So when execution leaves a scope, all automatic objects that were created in that scope are destroyed. Listed below are the control statements that are supported by Python –

a) **Break statement** – it ends the current loop statement and transfers execution to the statement immediately following the loop. The break statement can be used in both *for* and *while* loops. Most common use of break statement is when some external condition is triggered requiring a quick exit from loop.
Syntax-
break

b) **Continue statement** – The control is returned to the beginning of the while loop. The continue statements reject all the remaining statements in the current iteration of the loop and moves the control back to the top of the loop. It can be used for both *for* and *while* loops.
Syntax-
continue

c) **Pass statement** – When a statement is required syntactically but you do not want any command or code to execute, we use pass statement. It is a *null* operation and nothing happens on execution.
Syntax –
pass

STRINGS

In python, strings can be created by simply enclosing characters in quotes. The single quotes are treated same as double quotes. It is as easy as assigning value to a variable. Python has a built-in string called as 'str' which has many features. A literal in string can expand into multiple lines but there has to be back slash at the end of each line before the new line is created.

Example –
var 1 = 'Goodmorning World!'
var 2 = ' Python Programming'

How to access values in strings?

A character type is not supported by Python, they are considered as strings of length one, therefore also considered as substring. In order to access substring, the square brackets are used for slicing along with the index or indices.

Example –
var 1 = 'Goodmorning World!'
var 2 = "Python Programming"
print "var1[0]:", var1[0]
print "var2[1:5]:", var2[1:5]

result –
var1[0]: G
var2[1:5]: ytho

Updating Strings

Existing strings can be updated by (re)assigning a variable to another string. The new value can be related to a completely different string altogether or to its previous value.

String operators

There are various string operators, assume variable **a** holds 'Hello' and **b** holds 'World'

Operator	Description	Example
*	Repetition –it prints the character twice.	a*2 will give HelloHello
+	Concatenation- adds value on both sides and gives results	a + b will give Hello World
[:]	Range slice – gives characters from given range.	a[1:4] will give ell
[ ]	Slice – gives characters from given index	a[1]will give e
not in	Membership – if a character does not exist in a given string it returns true	M not in a will give 1
in	Membership – if character exists in the given string it returns true	H in a will give 1
r/R	Raw string- it surpasses actual meaning of escape characters	Print r'\n' prints \n and print R'\n' prints \n
%	Format – does string formatting	Read below

<u>String formatting</u>
The string formatting % operator is exclusive to strings and makes up for the bunch of having functions from C's printf family.

Example –
print "My name is %s and weight is %d kg!" % ('Alex', 25)

Result –
My name is Alex and weight is 25kg!

<u>Triple Quotes</u>

A triple quote in Python allows the strings to span in multiple lines which include verbatim TABs, NEWLINEs, and many other special characters. The syntax for triple quotes include three consecutive double or single   quotes.

Changing lower and upper case

In Python, you can change the string to upper case from lower case

str = "this is an example";
print "str.capitalize( ):", str.upper( )

Result –
str.capitalize( ): THIS IS AN EXAMPLE

LISTS

In Python, the fundamental data structure is a sequence. All the elements in a sequence are assigned a number; its index or position. In python, there are six built-in types of sequences and most common are tuples and lists.
Lists are the most flexible data type which can be written as a list of values separated by comma between the square brackets. The items in the list may not be of same type.

Example –
list 1 = ['english', 'french', 1996, 2015];
list2 = [1, 2, 3, 4, 5];
list3 = ["x", "y", "z"]

Just like string indices, list indices also start at 0, and list can be concatenated, sliced and so on.

How to access values in lists?

The square brackets are used for slicing along with the indices or index to get a value at the index.

list 1 = ['english', 'french', 1996, 2015];
list2 = [1, 2, 3, 4, 5, 6, 7];
print "list1[0]:", list1[0]

print "list2[1:5]:", list2[1:5]
Result –

list1[0]: English
list2[1:5]: [2, 3, 4, 5]

<u>Updating Lists</u>

Multiple elements or a single element of lists can be updated by giving the slice on the left-hand side of the assignment operator. It is possible to add elements in a list by using the append( ) method.

Example –

list = ['english', 'french', 1996, 2015];
print "Value available at index 2:"
print list[2]
list[2] = 2016;
print "New value available at index 2:"
print list[2]

Result –

Value available at index 2:
1996
New value available at index 2:
2016

<u>Deleting elements from list</u>

By using either the remove( ) method if you don't know which element to delete or del statement if you know exactly which element(s) you are deleting you can delete a list element.

Example –

list = ['english', 'french', 1996, 2015];

print list1
del list1[2];

print "After deleting value at index 2:"
print list 1

Result-

['english', 'french', 1996, 2015]

After deleting value at index 2:
['english', 'french', 2015]
Similar to Strings, lists also react to * and + operators; they mean repetition and
concatenation here as well, except that the outcome is a new list, not a string. As
the lists are sequences, slicing and indexing also works in a similar manner as in
strings.

Python has some built-in list functions –
1. cmp(list1, list2) – it compares elements in each list
2. max(list) - it returns item from the list with maximum value.
3. len(list) – it gives total strength of the list.
4. min(list)- it returns items from the list with minimum value.
5. List(seq) – it converts tuple into list.

List methods –
1. list.append(obj)- it appends object obj to list
2. list.extend(seq) – it appends the contents of seq to list
3. list.count(obj) – it returns count of how many times obj occurs in list.
4. list.insert(index,obj) – it inserts obj into list at offset index.
5. list.index(obj)- it returns the lowest index in the list that obj appears.
6. list.remove(obj) – it removes object from list
7. list.pop(obj=list[-1])- it removes and returns the last obj from list.
8. list.sort([func]) – sorts objects of list, use compare function if given
9. list.reverse( )- it reverses object of list in place.

TUPLES

The series of unchangeable Python objects are called as tuples. They are
sequences similar to lists. Unlike lists, you cannot change tuples and they make
use of parentheses, on the other hand square brackets are used in lists. You can
create tuples by simply separating values with a comma and optionally these
values which are separated by comma can be put inside parentheses.

Example –

tup1 = ('english', 'french', 1996, 2015);
tup2 = (1, 2, 3, 4, 5);
tup3= "x", "y", "z";

Two parentheses consisting of nothing; tup= ( ); denotes an empty tuple.

In order to write tuple that contains single value a comma needs to be included, even though there is barely a single value; tup1= (45,);

How to access values in Tuples?

Make use of the square brackets for slicing, besides the index or indices to get the value available at the index.

Example –
tup1 = ('english', 'french', 1996, 2015);
tup2 = (1, 2, 3, 4, 5, 6, 7);

print "tup1[0]:", tup1[0]
print "tup2[1:5]:", tup2[1:5]

result –

tup1[0]: English
tup2[1:5]: [2, 3, 4, 5]

How to update tuples?

Since tuples are unchangeable you cannot change or update the tuple elements values. You can take parts of existing tuple to make new tuples.

Example –

Tup1 = (14, 32.44);
Tup2 = ('xyz', 'abc');

```
#Below action is not valid for tuples
#tup1[0] =100;
```

```
# Therefore let's create a new tuple
```

```
tup3 = tup1 + tup2;
print tup3
```

result –

(14, 32.44, 'xyz', 'abc')

<u>Deleting elements in tuples</u>

Individual elements of tuples cannot be removed. However, there is nothing wrong in positioning together one more tuple with the undesired elements discarded. In order to completely remove a tuple, just add **del** statement.

Example –

tup = ('english', 'french', 1996, 2015);

```
print tup
del tup;
print "After deleting tup:"
print tup
```

Result –

('english', 'french', 1996, 2015)

After deleting tup:
Traceback (most recent call last):
 file "test.py", line 9, in <module>
  print tup;
NameError: name 'tup' is not defined

Please note that an exception is raised because after del tup tuple does not exist.

Similar to strings, tuples react to * and + operators; they denote repetition and concatenation here too, but a new tuple is created as a result and not a string. The indexing and slicing in tuples works in a similar way as it works in strings.

Following are the built-in functions of tuples –

1. cmp(tuple1, tuple2) – it compares the elements in each tuple
2. max(tuple) – it returns item from the tuple with maximum value.
3. len(tuple) – it gives the total length of the tuple.
4. tuple(seq)- it converts a list into a tuple.
5. min(tuple) – it returns item from the tuple with minimum value.

PYTHON DICTIONARY

Dictionary values can be of any kind, but the keys must be of an unchangeable data type such as numbers, strings and tuples.

How to access values in Dictionary?

By using the square brackets along with the key to obtain its value dictionary elements can be accessed.

Example –

dict = {'Name': 'Tom', 'Age': 10, 'Class': 'Fifth'}
print "dict['Name']:", dict['Name']
print "dict['Age']:", dict['Age']

Result –

dict['Name']: Tom
dict['Age']: 10

Properties of Dictionary Keys

a) Per key you cannot have more than one entry, i.e. duplicate key is not allowed. The preceding assignment wins when a duplicate key is encountered.

b) Keys should be unchangeable. By this it means that you may utilize numbers, strings or tuples as dictionary keys but something like ['key'] is not allowed.

Built-in dictionary functions-

1. cmp(dict1,dict2) – compares elements in both
2. str(dict)- produces a printable string
3. len(dict) – gives total length of dictionary
4. type(variable) – returns the type of passed variable.

Built-in dictionary methods-

1. dict.clear( ) – removes all elements of dictionary
2. dict.fromkeys( )- creates a new dictionary with keys from seq and values set to value
3. dic.copy( ) – returns a shallow copy of dictionary
4. dict.get(key, default=None) – returns value or default if key not in dictionary.
5. dict.has_key(key) – returns true if key in dictionary*dict*, otherwise false
6. dict.keys( )- returns list of dictionary dict's keys
7. dict.items( ) – returns a list of *dict's* tuple pairs
8. dict.setfedault(key,default=None) – similar to get, but will set dict[key]= default if *key* is not already in dict.
9. dict.values( )- returns list of dictionary *dict's* values.
10. dict.update( )- adds dictionary *dict2's* key-values pair to *dict*

Chapter 5: Insight into Python Functions, Modules and Classes

FUNCTIONS

A block of code that is organized, reusable, and is used to carry out a single, related action is called as a function. The functions provide better modularity for your application and a high degree of code reusing. Python has many built-in functions but creating your own functions is also possible and these are called as *user-defined* functions.

How to define a Function?

In order to give the necessary functionality you can define a function. Here, are some simple rules for defining a function in Python –
1. A function block begins with the keyword def followed by the function name and parentheses (( )).
2. Any arguments or input parameters must be positioned within these parentheses. Parameters can also be defined within these parentheses.
3. Inside every function the block of code starts with a colon and is indented.
4. The statement return [expression] exits a function, optionally passing back an expression to the caller. The return statement with no arguments is the same as return None.
5. The first statement of a function can be an optional statement; the documentation string of the function or *docstring*.

Syntax –
def functionname (parameters):
   "function_doctsring"
   function_suite
   return [expression]

Parameters, by default have a positional behavior and you need to inform them in the similar order as they were defined.

How to call a function?

By defining a function you only give a name to a function, structures the block of code and specify the parameters that are to be included in the function. Once the basic structure of a function is finalized, you can execute it by calling it from the Python prompt directly or from another function.

Example of function printme( ) is as below –

```
# Function definition is here
def printme(str):
    "This prints a passed string into this function"
    print str
    return;
```

```
# Call the printme function now
printme ("This is first call to user defined function!")
printme ("This is second call to the same function")
```

Output –
This is first call to user defined function!
This is second call to the same function

In Python, all parameters (arguments) are passed by reference. This means what a parameter refers to inside a function, if you change it, the change gets reflected back in the calling function.

Function Arguments

By using following types of arguments you can call a function –
   a) Required arguments –these are the arguments passed to a function in correct positional order. In this the number of arguments in the function call should exactly match with the function definition.
   b) Keyword arguments – These are related to function calls. Once keyword argument is used in a function call, the parameter name identifies the arguments to the caller. This allows for skipping of arguments or places them out of order since the keywords given to match the values with parameters is used by the Python interpreter.
   c) Default arguments –in the function call if a value is not provided for the argument this argument assumes a default value.
   d) Variable-length arguments – While defining a function it may be required to process a function for additional arguments than specified, these are

called as variable-length arguments. Unlike default and required arguments, they are not named in the function definition. The variable name that carries the value of all non-keyword variable arguments an asterisk is placed before it. Tuple will remain empty in case there are no extra arguments specified during a function call.

Scope of Variables

In a program, all variables may not be accessible at all locations. This depends on where you have declared a variable. The portion of the program where you can access a particular identifier is determined by the scope of variables. There are two basic scopes –

a) Global – Variables that are defined outside the function body have a global scope. These can be accessed throughout the program body by all functions.

b) Local – Variables that are defined inside the function body have a local scope. These can be accessed only inside a function in which they are declared.

MODULES

Modules help in organizing the code logically. The code becomes easy to use and understand by grouping the related code into module. A Python object with arbitrarily named attributes that can bind and reference is called module. In simple words, module is a file that consists of Python code. It can define variables, functions, and classes.

Example of simple module support.py -

```
def print_func( par ):
    print " Hi:", par
    return
```

Import Statememt

Any Python source file can be used as a module by executing an import statement in some other Python source file.

Syntax –

34

import module1[, module2[,. . .moduleN]

From import statement

Specific attributes can be imported from a module into the current namespace
with the help of *from import* statements.

Syntax –
from modname import name1[, name2[,. . .nameN]]

From...import * statement

The *from..import*statement* makes the import of all names possible from a
module into the current namespace.

from modname import*

Locating Modules
The module is searched by the Python interpreter in the below mentioned
sequence when a module is imported.
   a) Current directory
   b) In case the module isn't found, the Python looks into every directory in the
      shell variable PYTHONPATH
   c) The default path is checked in Python, if else fails.

The module search path is stored in the system module sys as the
sys.pathvariable. This variable contains the current directory, PYTHONPATH,
and the installation dependent default.
PYTHONPATH – it is an environment variable, which consists of a list of
directories.
Syntax-
For windows -
set PYTHONPATH=c:\python20\lib;

For UNIX-
set PYTHONPATH=/usr/local/lib/python

Namespaces and scoping

A namespace is a dictionary of variable names (keys) and their corresponding objects (values)

Variable can be accessed in Python in both local and global namespace. In case a global and local variable has the same name, the global variable is overshadowed by the local variable. All functions have their own local namespace. The same scoping rules are followed by classes as ordinary functions. Whether variables are global or local is a informed guess made by Python. An assumption is made that any variable is local which has been assigned a value in a function. Therefore, for assigning a value to a global variable inside a function, the global statement needs to be used first. The statement *global VarName*tells that VarName is global. Searching the local namespace for the variable is stopped by Python.

The dir( ) function-

It returns a systematic list of strings consisting of the names defined by a module. List consists of all the functions, modules and variables that are defined in a module.

The globals( ) and locals( ) functions-

These functions can be used to return names in the local and local namespaces depending on the location from where they are called. If from inside a function a globals( ) is called, it will return all the names that can be globally accessed from that function. In case locals( ) is called from inside a function, it will return names that can be locally accessed from that function. The return type for both the functions is dictionary. So the names can be extracted using the keys( ) function.

The reload( ) function

The code in the top level portion of a module is executed only once when the module is imported into a script. However, if you want to execute the top level code again, then use the reload( ) function. A previously imported module is imported again by this function.

Syntax –

reload(module_name)

In syntax, *module_name* is the name of the module to be reloaded and not the string consisting of the module name.

CLASSES

As we know that Python is an object-oriented language, therefore using and creating objects and classes is easy. A class is a user-defined model for an object that defines a set of attributes that portray any object of the class. The attributes are the data members and methods, associated via dot notation. Data member is an instance variable or a class variable that holds data related with a class and its objects. The instance variable is a variable that is defined inside a method and belongs to the current instance of a class.

How to create classes?

A new class definition is created by a *class* statement. The name of the class straight away follows the keyword *class* followed by a colon.

class ClassName:
　　'Optional class documentation string'
　　class_suite
- A class has a documentation string, which can be accessed via ClassName._doc_.
- Each component statement that defines class members, functions and data attributes exist in the *class_suite*.

How to create instances of class?

Use class name to call the class and pass in no matter what arguments its *_init_* method accepts for creating an instance of a class.

How to access attributes?

Dot operator with object need to be used in order to access the object's attributes.

Built-in class attributes

Dot operator can be used to access the built-in attributes–

37

a) _dict_ - dictionary containing class's namespace
b) _name_ - class name
c) _doc_ - class documentation string or none, if undefined.
d) _bases_ - probably a vacant tuple containing the base classes in the order of their occurrence in the base class list.
e) _module_ - the module name in which class is defined. This attribute in interactive mode is "_main_".

Garbage Collection

In Python, to make the memory space free, objects (class instances or built-in) that are not required are deleted automatically. Garbage collection is a method by which Python from time to time recovers memory blocks that are no longer in use. Python's garbage collector runs while the program is being executed and is triggered when an object's reference count reaches zero. An object's reference count increases when it is positioned in a container (tuple, list or dictionary) or is assigned a new name. The object's reference count decreases when it is deleted with *del,* its reference goes out of scope or it is reassigned. Python automatically collects when an object's reference count reaches zero.

Class inheritance

A pre-existing class can be used for deriving and creating a new class instead of begining from scratch by listing the parent class after the new class name inside parentheses. The attributes of its parent class are inherited by the child class, and these attributes can be used as if they were defined in the child class. Just like their parent class the derived classes can be declared. Though, after the class name a list of base classes to inherit from is given.

Syntax –

class SubClassName (ParentClass1[, ParentClass2,. . .]):
    'Optional class documentation string'
    class_suite (Python - Environment Setup)

Chapter 6: Exception handling

Exception

An event that interrupts the standard flow of the program's instructions at the time of execution is called as an exception. Typically, when such a situation is encountered by a Python script that it cannot handle, it raises an exception. In other words, an exception is a Python object that depicts an error. When an exception is raised in Python script, it either the exception is handled immediately or it is terminated.

How to handle an exception?

In case you find a suspicious code in a program, then the program can be defended by putting that code in a **try:** block. After this include an **except:**statement followed by a block of code which manages the problem as gracefully as possible.

Syntax –

try:
  You do your operations here;
  ....
except Exception I:
  If there is Exception I, then execute this block.
Except Exception II:
  If there is Exception II, then execute this block.
  ....
else:
  If there is no exception then execute this block.

Please note –
- A single try statement can have multiple except statements.
- A generic except clause can also be provided, which manages any exception.
- An else-clause can also be included after except clause(s). If the code in try: block does not raise an exception the code in the else-block is executed.

- A better place for code that does not need the try: block's protection is the else-block.

Except Clause with no exception –all the exceptions that occur are caught by the try-except statement. However, it doesn't make the programmer recognize the root cause of the problem that may occur.

Except clause with multiple exceptions- the same except statement to handle multiple exceptions can be used.

Try-finally clause – The finally: block with try: block can be used. In the finally block you can place any code that must execute, irrespective of the fact that the try-block has raised an exception or not.

Argument of an exception – An argument is a value that gives more information about the problem and an exception can have an argument. You can catch an exception's argument by providing a variable in the except clause.

Raising Exceptions

You can raise exceptions in several ways by using the raise statement.

Syntax –

raise [Exception [, args [, traceback]]]

Here, *argument* is a value for the exception argument and *Exception* is the type of exception. However, argument is optional; if not supplied, the exception argument is None. For example, an exception can be a class, string or an object. Most exceptions that Python core raises are classes, with an argument that is an instance of the class.

In Python, you are allowed to create your own exceptions by deriving classes from the standard built-in exceptions. (Python Exceptions Handeling)

Conclusion

This brings us to the end of this edition of the book. We can easily say that Python is a powerful language and that is the reason why all big companies are looking for programmers who have the knowledge of this dynamic language.

Before we end, let's summarize on what we have learned so far. The book began with basic introduction to Python, its features, how to install and set up. We also understood that Python has fewer syntactical constructs thus making it easy and readable. All Python fundamentals i.e. variables, data types, operators, lists, strings, loops, tuples and dictionary have been covered in the book.

We have also ensured that the concept of function, classes, and modules is covered for a better understanding of the language. The last section on exception handling can be useful in practical application.

To conclude, we can say that once you are clear on the basics of Python you will be able to create almost anything you want.

Thank you once again for downloading this book, hope it has given you a meaningful insightinto Python.

Works Cited

Python - Environment Setup. n.d. 2017.
    <https://www.tutorialspoint.com/python/python_environment.htm>.

Python Exceptions Handeling. n.d. 2017.
    <https://www.tutorialspoint.com/python/python_exceptions.htm>.

Book 2

Fortran Crash Course

By: PG WIZARD BOOKS

*Step By Step Guide To Mastering Fortran
Programming!*

Fortran Crash Course: Step By Step Guide To Mastering Fortran
Programming!

Table of Contents

Fortran Crash Course: Step By Step Guide To Mastering Fortran
Programming!

Introduction

Many beginners to coding worry that they are not going to be able to learn
how to work with a new coding language. They feel that it is going to be too
difficult to learn the language and that they will either not be able to do
some of the programming that they want or that they just won't
understand what is being said in the information. But when it comes to
working with Fortran, you will find that learning how to code is a simple
process.

In this guidebook, we are going to start out by talking about some of the
information that comes with Fortran. We will also work on the first code
for this language and discuss all the different parts that are going to be
found inside of your code. This is a simple introduction to help you get
some practice with writing your own code and ensures that you are able to
get into some of the more complex situations that we will discuss later on.

Once we have these basics down, we are going to move on to some of the
other things that you are able to do when it comes to working on your code
in Fortran. We will take a look at writing some of your own loop
statements, what strings and arrays are, working with conditional
statements, and so much more. Even as a beginner, you will be able to use
these options in order to make a really strong code and program as you
want it.

When you are ready to get into coding and want to make sure that you are
designing something that is strong and will work the way that you want,
Fortran is one of the best coding languages to help you learn how to get it
done. Make sure to use this guidebook to help you to get the basics to work
with Fortran for all your coding needs.

Chapter 1: Learning the Basics of Fortran

As a beginner, you may have times that you are worried that a new coding language will be too hard for you to learn. You want to make your own programs, learn how to work in different operating systems, or have another goal that you would like to accomplish, but you worry that it is going to be too much work for you to accomplish because it will be too hard to do. But when it comes to learning how to work with Fortran (which is basically a contraction of Formula Translation), you are working with a great language that is designed for beginners, even for those that have no experience in coding before.

Fortran is considered one of the oldest programming languages that you can use and this can be a benefit as well as an issue. It is beneficial because you will be able to find this language anywhere that you want to look and the compiler, as well as the other add-ons, are all going to be free. It is a coding language that many scientists and engineers like to use because of all the functions that are built in and the fact that it is easily used with mathematical constructs. There are also many other things that you are able to do with this coding language, and since it is one of the oldest options around, you are sure to find lots of help and answers to ensure that you get the project done right.

What will I need to get started?

When you are ready to get started with Fortran, you will need to bring out a new text editor. There are several of these that are available, and you can choose the one that works for you. You need this because it allows you to out the codes so that the compiler, which you will need next, will be able to read out what you are doing and tell the computer how to behave. You are not able to use a word processor for this because these kinds of applications are not going to save files in plain text, which is required to make the compiler do its job.

Next on the list is the compiler. There are many options out there and most of them are going to be free as well so you can download these and not have to worry about adding in costs. Basically the compiler is going to take the words that you have written in the text editor and then change them

47

around into something that the computer is actually able to read. You will just need to save your code and then the compiler will be able to execute it.

Some people find that working with an Integrated Development Environment, or IDE, is a great way to help make this a lot easier. This IDE is going to work similar to the text editor and the compiler in one so it saves you some time, especially when it comes to troubleshooting the written code. For those who are working on Windows computers, the IDE is really a good idea because it has an interface that is easy to sue and similar to what you are used to seeing on the Windows computer.

As mentioned, you could just use the text editor and the compiler, but the IDE does make it a bit easier to write your code. These combine both of the other two products in one and it is able to understand syntaxes of the code easily. In fact, it is going to be able to catch some of the errors that come up in the code as you are typing, saving a lot of time and accidents in the process.

The benefits of using Fortran for your coding

There are so many reasons why you may want to consider using Fortran as your coding language of choice. Whether you are looking to use it on the side as another coding language to master or this is one of the first coding languages that you are going to work with, the benefits of choosing this one are amazing. Some of the reasons that you would want to work with the Fortran coding language include:

- Easy to use: Fortran was designed for the beginner to learn how to use it. It is a simple language to work with and after looking at some of the codes in this book, you are sure to see that it is easy enough to learn how to work with.
- Has been around for a long time: Fortran is one of the first coding languages that came available for coders to use in their homes. This is a good thing because it is simplistic and easy to use. We are going to work on a few different codes inside of this guidebook and you will find that most of them are pretty straight forward and easy to write, even if you are a beginner. While some people feel that the fact that Fortran has been around for so long is a bad thing, it can mean so

many good things for helping you to get the very best when working in coding.

- Great for the scientific community: this is a language that anyone is able to use for their own needs, but it is specifically important when it comes to the scientific community. If you have an occupation that is in this field, you will find that it is a good idea to learn how to use the Fortran code.
- Lots of programs still use it: even though this is an older coding language that you can use, there are still a lot of programs that use it. This means that you will have plenty of chances to use this programming language and to get some more practice.
- Can be modified for other languages: Fortran is one of the earliest coding languages that is out there so it has had many adaptations over the years. This means that there are versions that you are able to use and combine with some of your other programming languages. This makes it easier to do some of the more powerful things that you want to do with your coding.
- It is free: all the stuff that you need for Fortran, from the software itself to the IDE that you want to use with it, is all free to use. This makes it easier for everyone to use this language because you won't have to worry about all the costs that are associated with it.
- Has a big community: when it comes to using a brand new language, you want to make sure that you have a community that is able to answer your questions and make sure that you going on the right track. Since Fortran has been around for so long, there are many people who know how to use this and can be there to help you out.

There are many benefits to using the Fortran coding language. While some people prefer to go with another option that is easier or newer to use, there are still many people who want to work with Fortran because it is one of the first. It is a simplistic language to learn how to use even as a beginner, and it is able to get a lot of the coding and programming done that you would like. If you are looking for a coding language that is pretty easy to work with and is meant for beginners, you won't go wrong when choosing Fortran.

How to test my first code

Now that we have spent some time talking about the things that you need
to get started with the Fortran coding, it is time to test out one of our first
codes. Once you have taken the time to install the IDE that you would like
to use, it is time to double click on the icon so that the programming
environment is going to open up. You can then create a brand new file but
keep in mind that you may need to select on a Fortran file when you do
this, just in case the IDE that you picked is able to read more than one
language. So you will need to give it the extension of .f95 rather than of .txt
so that you are able to compile these statements a bit later on.

One thing to keep in mind is that there are some other extensions that you
are able to use when it comes to Fortran including .FOR, .F, and FPP.
These extensions are going to tell the compiler was standards you are
following with the work you do so make sure that you pick the one that you
want and stick with it. You can experiment a bit to figure out which one you
want to use.

So once you are done picking out the extension that you would like to use
(we are going to stick with the .f95 one for now), we are going to need to
type out the following code to get started:

program mytest

!this is a test

Print *, 'This is an output test'

end program mytest

After we have taken the time to type out this bit of code, it is time to
execute it inside of the IDE. Your compiler will then go through and double
check the parts of the code, looking to see if you have made any errors in
the code before trying to run it. If there are any errors that show up, the
IDE will let you know and ask you to fix it. If there aren't any troubles with
the code, the compiler is going to generate and then execute the file.
Basically, with this one you are going to find that the words "This is an
output test" will show up on the screen if you typed it in the right way.

Breaking down this code

Now that we have taken some time to write our own code, it is time to break it down to make a bit more sense. Like a lot of the other coding languages that are out there, the Fortran language is going to take care of the different lines of the code, which are called statements, and then decide what it is going to do with each of them. So in the first line, the program is going to state the name of the program that you are trying to work with.

Then moving on to the second line, you are working with a comment. This basically means that you are writing a little note for yourself or for the other programmers that are taking a look at the code. The compiler knows that it shouldn't execute the comment since this is just a little note. You can add in as many comments as you would like inside of the code to describe what the different parts are going to do.

The third line of the code is the output command that is going to tell the compiler what it is supposed to display on the screen. It is going to show up in a single quote. You can make this statement as long or short as you would like, just make sure that you are using the right options with it. And then in the last line, the statement is terminating, or ending, the program that you just write.

Now, this is a pretty basic option that we are working on and only has four lines. There are many options that you are able to do with Fortran that will use more lines to get it done depending on the things that you are doing inside the code. There are also a few versions of Fortran that will have the code look a bit different. Basically all of them need to have the four same parts including the program name, the output statements (you may have more than one of these in some cases), end of program, and comments if you need them.

Making sure that you have all the right parts in place in order to write the code is important to helping the compiler to work with you on creating the code. And while there are many different data types that you are able to use, as we will discuss as we go on in this guidebook, they can be as simple or as difficult as you need to make the code work.

Chapter 2: Working on Loops in Fortran

When you are working on writing your own code inside of Fortran, you need to understand how to work with loops. There are many different times when you will want the code to keep repeating something, or do a specific action more than once. With the most basic form of your code, you would need to write this part of the code over and over again. Now, if you just want the code to repeat a few times, this may not seem like such a big deal, but what happens when you want to write out the code 100 times? Rewriting the same part 100 times can get tiring and old pretty quickly.

But with loops, you are able to tell the compiler to repeat the same steps until the conditions are no longer true. This could be five times and it could be 1000 times, but you would just need to write out a few lines of code to make this happen. Rather than having to write out the same instructions over and over again, you are able to set up the loop to do the same functions over and over again.

There are several different components that are going to be found inside of a loop to make sure that it is going to work. The main components include:

- Step: this component is going to tell the compiler that the procedure will need to be repeated at least once.
- Start: this is going to tell the compiler that it is at the beginning of your loop.
- Stop: this is going to tell the compiler that it is at the end of your loop.
- Var: this is a variable. It is in charge of telling the compiler how many times that you would need to have your code repeated.

How do these loops work?

Loops are going to begin when you set the start and then you define the var. they will explore what concept you are working with inside the var and decide when the conditions have no longer been met so this will all start. As soon as your statement is executed once, the amount to the var is going to go up by one so that you don't end up in an endless loop. So, if you want to make a table that goes from one to ten, the var would start at one and then each time it goes up by one until it reaches ten. Let's take a look at a sample code that shows how the loop function is going to work:

```fortran
program loop_factorial

implicit none


      !definition of variables

      Integer::xfact=1

      Integer::x


      !computations of factorials

      Do x=1, 15

            Xfact=xfact*1

            Write*, x, xfact

      End do

End program loop_factorial
```

This one is a bit longer than what we are used to with the other code we wrote, but it does show how the loop is going to work for you. This one is going to make sure that the variable will keep going up by one each time that you work with it, helping to keep things organized and to ensure that you don't end up in an endless loop. If you do end up with a loop that doesn't have a stop point, you are going to get stuck inside of the code and have trouble getting out without closing the whole program.

There are a few different types of loops that you are able to work with. Some are going to check the conditions of the statement before determining whether or not to run the loop. If the conditions are not true from the beginning, you are not going to get the loop to run at all and it is going to head on to the next part of the code. This is known as the for loop. And then the do while loop is going to run the loop at least one time, and then run check the options to see if it meets the condition. The choice can be the same, but it does depend on whether you want the code to run one time or it doesn't matter.

The loop is one of the best things that you can work with when trying to make your code look nice and organized when on Fortran. You will be able to tell the loop how many times you would like it to run through the program, just using a few lines rather than rewriting the code all of the time. This is an efficient way to work inside of your code and ensures that the code is still able to work properly.

Chapter 3: Working with Strings and Arrays

When you are working with Fortran, you will find that strings and arrays
are great ways to help keep the code organized. There are certain ways that
you will be able to work with these in order to get them to execute inside of
the code properly. In this chapter, we are going to spend some time talking
about what strings and arrays are and how you would be able to work with
them inside your code.

What are strings?

Inside of the Fortran code, all characters are going to be seen as one of two
elements. They are seen as either single characters or contiguous strings.
So what is the difference between them? With a contiguous string, you will
notice that their length for syntax declaration is going to be passed, they
will allow you to do notations on the substring, they won't allow you to do
notation on arrays, they can contain descriptors if needed, and in some
cases there are going to be hidden arguments inside.

When you want to declare a string inside of Fortran, you are going to use
rules that are similar to declaring some of the other variables. So in order
to do this, you would use the following option (we are giving the string an
assignment of 10):

specifier :: variable_name

character(len=10)::name

Now in addition to working on the string, you will be able to work on
substrings, which are basically just smaller parts of the string. They are
going to be any part of the program that is executed and you are able to
extract them if you wish. For example, if you have a long string that is
several sentences long, you could work on a substring and just take out a
few of the words to make it easier to read if you want. Here is an example
of how you would be able to take out substrings from the string inside the
code:

```
program string_concatenation

implicit non


        character (len=5) :: name

        character (len=50) :: announcement

        character (len=50) :: message


        name = 'Dana Caulfield'

        announcement = 'This is'

        message = 'I would like to give you a warm welcome to Prescott
Academy!'


print *, announcement, name

print * , message

end program string_concatenation
```

With this option you are going to get the message "This is Dana Caulfield. I would like to give you a warm welcome to Prescott Academy!" You are able to choose how much of the message you would like to do and you can keep it all on one line or on more than one. For example, you could choose to just have "This is Dana Caulfield" show up on the screen if you would like. This gives you some options to have a longer phrase there if you would like while also keeping it so that you get smaller patches as well.

Concatenation

Another thing that we are going to take a look at when working inside of Fortran is known as concatenation. You are going to notice that it will use the (//) symbol in order to show that this is inside the code. The concatenation property is the one that describes which programs are able to link back to each other. Because of these connections that are established, the main goal is to either draw attention over to another branch in the program, or to make sure that the framework is solid. In some cases the links are going to be for two separate programs, but often the subjects are going to be single elements.

You can also work with a process that is known as trimming. This is when you want to cut out parts of the line that are not necessary so that you get the right result to show up. Since there can often be elements inside the program that aren't needed and are known as trailing blanks, the process of trimming is going to help to get rid of some of this clutter so that you are able to just use the portions that are needed. It also helps your compiler to be able to read through the code faster.

There are a lot of things that you are able to do with the strings inside of your projects and you will be able to mess around with them a bit to get the strings to work out the way that you want. But using concatenation and trimming will help to ensure that you are using the strings in the proper manner.

Arrays

Arrays are another important part of working on your code. They are going to be in charge of storing information, such as variables and characters, that are similar. If the piles of data aren't stored in the proper way, it is going to be really hard for the computer to be able to interpret them. However, when you use the arrays properly to put this information in the right places, the compiler is going to have a better chance at running the program and the functions will be executed in the proper way. Some of the things that you should remember about arrays to make it easier include:

- If you would like to specify the individual elements, you are going to need to address them using the subscripts. The first element is going to have the subscript of 1.
- If you see the term "extent" it is going to describe the elements that are along a dimension. Keep in mind that this is a numerical value.
- On the other hand, if you see the term rank, it is going to describe the dimensions that they have, using a numerical value as well.
- When you see the term "size" this is going to describe the elements that the array has, using numerical values again.
- The shape of the array is going to consist of elements.

- They are going to be declared with the attribute of dimension.
- They are going to be linked to memory locations that are contiguous.

There are two types of arrays that you are able to find inside of the Fortran language. The one-dimensional arrays are the ones that will serve as vectors while the two-dimensional arrays are the ones that will serve as the matrices.

Now that we know a little bit more about arrays, it is time to understand how you are going to be able to declare the arrays. Luckily this is a process that is pretty easy to complete. The rule is to specify the dimension that you desire, and then the compiler will be able to take a look at the elements that are involved and determine if they are an integer or real. For example, if you want to declare an array that is the Caulfield Lair and you want to give it seven elements, you would use the following code to make it happen:

real, dimension (7) :: Caulfield Lair.

Now you can also choose to declare an array that is two dimensional. Let's say that we are still using the example of Caulfield Lair from above, but we are going to make it so that the elements are 7 by 7. To do this, we are going to use the following syntax:

integer, dimension (7, 7) :: Caulfield Lair.

If you would like to make sure that you are assigning the right values to your arrays, you will find that the process is pretty simple. You just need to work on the array and then enter in the amount that you would like to use. You do have some choices when it comes to doing this because you can either do it on a single element that you want to change or you can work it out on the whole array. Let's take a look at an example of how this would work. Let's say that we want to add in the value of 3 to all of the elements would need the following code:

do I = 1, 7

Caulfield Lair = i*3.0

end program do.

But on the other hand, if you would like to assign the value of 3 to just the first level of the array and then add different numbers to the other levels, you would need to use the following code to make it happen:

Caulfield Lair (1) = 3

Working with strings and arrays are a good way to make sure that you are getting the code to work in the right way. The strings are going to be statements that happen inside the code and make it easier for you to write out the different things that you would like to have happen, either by adding in the whole string to the code or just having a few parts as you see fit. The arrays are going to be responsible for holding large pieces of data in a way that is easier to look through and reach inside the code. Both of these are going to be important to ensuring that you get more out of the code and that it works the way that you want.

Chapter 4: Manipulating the Variable Amounts

Now at this point we are going to take some time to look at the different operators and variables that you are able to use inside of your code. So far at this point we have learned a bit about how to create a simple program. But there is a lot of manipulation that you are can do inside the code and operators are a great way to help you to do this. The operators inside of Fortran is going to be a great way to do mathematical functions while also getting these results to show up on the screen. With all that we have learned so far about this program, it is now possible to work on a short program on our own that will help to manipulate the amounts of variables. So basically inside of this chapter, we are going to learn how to make our program in Fortran do some basic math.

First we need to take a look at what the variable is all about. A variable is basically a little container that is going to store information inside of the memory of the computer. You are able to use these to hold either one or more value of your choice, and you are able to assign this either at the beginning of your block of code or when the code is being executed.

Assigning a variable is going to be pretty easy to accomplish. You will just need to use the (=) in order to pick the value that you would like to use along with the variable. You are able to add more than one value to the same variable if you would like to store them together in the code, but for the most part, it is just going to be one variable that you are working with. You can add in many different variables inside of the code, but the operators that we are going to talk about in a minute help to make it easier to get this all done.

Before we get too far into making this kind of program, we are going to take some time to work with operators. While these are pretty simple, there are some times when they can seem confusing and will make you wonder what they mean. The trick with these is to not think of them as mathematical symbols. For example, when it comes to writing out a = 2, you should see this as the value of 2 is going to be stored inside the memory of your computer that is labeled as a. Here is another example that you can use:

a = 2

b = 3

c = a + b

In the statement that we did above, you will see that the value of 2 is going to be stored as the memory location that is a and then you will see that the value of 3 is stored in the memory location that is called be. And then when you add the values of a and b together, you are going to store that result under the memory location of c. Keep in mind with this one that you are not able to write out this kind of equation as a + b = c because the compiler is going to see this as an error. The one variable needs to be on the left-hand side of your symbol and then you can have as many of the variables as you would like on the right-hand side, but mixing these around are going to cause an error message.

Arithmetic operators

Now that we have looked at some examples of operators, it is time to work with some of the operators that you need. Not all of the math symbols that you will need are going to show up on the keyboard, but the Fortran does have some of its own symbols that you are able to use in order to represent the different math operands that you are able to use. Some of the most common arithmetic operators that you are able to use on your language includes:

- (+): this is the one that you are going to use for addition
- (-): this is the one that you are going to use for subtraction in the code.
- (*): this is the one that you are going to use for multiplication
- (/): this is the one that you can use for division

One thing to note with these is that you can use more than one of the symbols, whether you are using three addition signs or an addition and a division symbol, inside the same part of code. You are able to use as many of these as you want, but you need to use the order of operands to do it. This means that you will need to do all of the multiplication, then the division, addition, and subtraction, going from left to right to make sure that the compiler is going to give you the right answer.

Other parts of your code

As a beginner, you will wonder what all the blanks, or the skip positions, are inside of the program. Some people choose to write out their programs without using these at all, but for the most part, the programmers like to include these inside of their code in order to make it easier to read. You are able to choose how you would like to use a skip position, but you should include at least a few to make sure that your code is easier to read through.

There are also some special characters that you are able to work with inside of your code. These are used in order to deliver the function that you want. These are going to seem pretty simple and plain but you need to be careful about how you use them. If you use them the wrong way or place two of them into the code right next to each other, you could end up with conditions that cancel each other. Some of the special characters that are found inside of Fortran and that you should watch out for include:

- (/): this one is going to specify another line
- ("): to output strings
- (:): this is going to terminate a list
- () this is going to categorize the descriptors.

Descriptors can be a tool that you are able to use and they are variables that are going to specify the amount of data that is required for a conversion. It is a good idea to keep track of the usage of these since the process may not end unless you add in the right descriptor is placed inside. Some of the descriptors that you can use include:

- A: repetition
- D: this one is for digits next to your decimal points.
- E: this is for an exponential number
- M: this is the minimum amount of digits.
- W: this is width in total characters.

Fortran Crash Course: Step By Step Guide To Mastering Fortran
Programming!

You are going to be able to use all of these different parts to help you to get the code to work the way that you would like. You can mix and match a few of the parts to get the variable to be the right number, to store it in the right place inside the code and to do so much more. When you are able to add in the operators of the Fortran code, work with the blanks or the skip positions to make the code easier to use, and add in the special characters and the descriptors to the code, you are going to get a lot of power and options inside of the code.

Chapter 5: Working with Conditional Statements

At this point, we are going to take some time to look at the if statements. These are the most basic of the conditional statements and you will find that they are pretty straightforward. With this one, you will set the condition that needs to be met as well as the action that will show up at the same time with it. If the user puts in an input that matches, you will see that the program puts up the action that you choose. On the other hand, since this is a simple equation to work with, when the user puts in an input that is seen as false, the program is just going to end because you didn't set up an action.

So for this one, let's say that you just want people who are 18 to be able to get into the website. You would set up the if statement to accept any answer that is 18 and above. If the user places their age inside to be 20, the action (such a statement that you choose) will be executed by the compiler. But if the user puts in that their age is 16, then the program is going to see that this answer is false compared to the conditions that you set, and since you are using the if statement, nothing is going to happen.

Now there are some issues that can come up with this, but let's just focus on learning the syntax and getting this part down. Take a look at the syntax below for this:

if (x == 1) then

print *, 'turn left'

end if

The logical operator is the one that is used in this example along with the statement of if..then..end if. Note the expression that comes after the if statement. It is going to provide you with a test, something that is necessary when you are trying to imply a condition. In this case, we are going to assume that the "x" variable is an integer. One of the values that it can be is equal to 1. Interpreting this as a logical operation, the program is going to test to see if the value of the variable is 1. Then it will check if this is true or not. If your variable is 1, then the statements that come next will

64

be executed which in this case would be the words "turn left". Then the end
if is going to terminate the program that you are working on.

The if...else statements

As we mentioned in the last part, the if statement is going to be pretty basic
and there are some issues with it. Your user may very well be 16 years old
and it isn't a good idea to have the program just end if they put in this
answer. You most likely will want to have some message come up at least,
so that the user doesn't assume that something is wrong with the program.
For example, if they put that their age is over 18, you would want to set it
up to say something like "Welcome to the site!" and then have the next
action be that they can get in. But if they put in that they are 16 or
something else, you would rather have a message like "Only those over 18
are allowed in the game!" than having the program just end.

The if...else statement is able to help you to do that. You would set it up like
the first part that we had above, but then you would add the else that
catches anything that is considered false by the compiler based on the
conditions that you set. This allows you to have an answer, any answer,
come up regardless of what input the user is giving to you. This makes it
much more clean cut and easier to deal with and doesn't leave the user
wondering what is wrong with the user.

In addition, you are able to make it so that there are several options that
come up. Let's say that you would like to have someone pick out their
favorite color of either red, green, yellow, or blue. You would just need to
write out more of the else sections of this code would just keep going.
Another really useful thing for you to learn how to use inside of your
Fortran code is the conditional statement. These are really great because
they allow you to have some extra power and choices inside of the code.
These will allow you to put in the conditions that need to be met in order to
get different statements or actions to occur. They can be really simple, such
as the if statement, where you will only have an action happen when the
answer is inputted is true compared to your conditions, you can have it so
that a different action will happen based on if the answer is true or false
based on your condition, or you can give the user some choices.

You can decide what conditions need to be met before you allow the user to
put in their information. This allows the code to keep things simple and it
can look at your conditions before executing what you would like to have
happen. You can make these as complex or as simple as you would like, but
remember that you do need to base these on Boolean expressions. You

have to leave the answer as either true or false based on the conditions that
you set.

Don't worry if this sounds complicated right now. We are going to take
some time to look over the different conditional statements that you are
able to work with and help you to get the results that you want, no matter
what kind of conditional statement you are working with.

The if statements

down the line, taking a look through each condition and statement that you
put onto the screen. You can also add in a catch or break at the end so if the
user picks pink or another color that isn't listed there so they still get an
answer.

There are so many options that you are able to do with the if...else
statements and they can really open up a lot of what you are able to do
inside of your code. You can make them as simple or as complex as you
would like, adding in more sections or just having a true and false option.
Mess around with this a bit and see what you are able to come up with on
your if...else statements.

Conclusion

Working in a coding language can be difficult no matter who you are. Many beginners are worried that they are not going to be able to find the answers to getting started or that it is just going to be too hard for them to pick out how to work with this code. But when it comes to working in Fortran, you will find that writing out a code can be nice and simple and it won't take that long for you to learn it and start working on your own.

This guidebook is going to take some time to help you learn how to work with the Fortran code. We are going to start out with writing some of our own codes while learning about some of the basics that come with Fortran. We will then move on to working with strings and arrays, understanding how the loops work, and even working with conditional statements. These are actually really important parts of working with a coding language, but since Fortran is so simple to work with that you will be able to add them into a code in no time.

When you are ready to get started on writing some of your own codes and want to get into the world of coding, working with Fortran is one of the best options to help you to get this all done. It is an older language that is meant for beginners and you will be able to catch on to it in no time at all. Use this guidebook to learn what you need to know in order to get the Fortran language to work for you.